Building a Home in Space

James Bow

CRABTREE
PUBLISHING COMPANY
WWW.CRABTREEBOOKS.COM

Author: James Bow

Editors: Sarah Eason, Tim Cooke,
Ellen Rodger

Editorial director: Kathy Middleton

Design: Paul Myerscough, Lynne Lennon

Cover design: Paul Myerscough

Photo research: Rachel Blount

Proofreader and indexer: Nancy Dickmann,
Wendy Scavuzzo

**Production coordinator
and prepress technician:** Ken Wright

Print coordinator: Katherine Berti

Consultant: David Hawksett

Produced for Crabtree Publishing by Calcium Creative

Photo Credits:
t=Top, tr=Top Right, tl=Top Left

Inside: NASA: pp. 10, 14, 20, 23, 31, 32, 40; NASA Ames Research Center/Rick Guidice: p. 44; NASA/Ricky Arnold: p. 41; NASA/ESA/K. Retherford/SWRI: p. 7; NASA/JPL-Caltech: p. 38; NASA/JPL-Caltech/Space Science Institute: p. 39; Lockheed Martin: p. 34; NASA/Frank Michaux: p. 24; NASA/Soyuz TMA-21: p. 11; NASA/Carla Thomas: p. 25; Shutterstock: 3Dsculptor: pp. 16, 35; Alfazet Chronicles: p. 45b; Curraheeshutter: p. 9; Elenarts: p. 8; Eric Isselee: p. 6; Dotted Yeti: p. 45t; Wikimedia Commons: Neil Armstrong: p. 12; Diliff: p. 43; Hbarrison: p. 28; Ittiz: p. 26; D Mitriy: p. 30; NASA: pp. 13, 15, 27, 33, 37, 42; NASA Ames Research Center: p. 5; NASA/Crew of Expedition 8: p. 19; NASA (Crew of Skylab 4): pp. 1, 17; NASA/Crew of STS-132: p. 18; NASA/Dennis M. Davidson: p. 22; NASA Earth Observatory: p. 4; NASA / JHU/APL: p. 36; NASA/Pat Rawlings: pp. 21, 29.

Cover: Shutterstock: Pavel Chagochkin.

Library and Archives Canada Cataloguing in Publication

Bow, James, author
      Building a home in space / James Bow.

(Mission: space science)
Includes index.
Issued in print and electronic formats.
ISBN 978-0-7787-5384-1 (hardcover).--
ISBN 978-0-7787-5397-1 (softcover).--
ISBN 978-1-4271-2206-3 (HTML)

    1. Space colonies--Juvenile literature.
2. Outer space--Civilian use--Juvenile literature. I. Title.

TL795.7.B69 2019   j629.44'2   C2018-906095-6
                                 C2018-906096-4

Library of Congress Cataloging-in-Publication Data

Names: Bow, James, author.
Title: Building a home in space / James Bow.
Description: New York, New York : Crabtree Publishing Company, [2019] | Series: Mission: space science | Includes index.
Identifiers: LCCN 2018050345 (print) | LCCN 2018050798 (ebook) | ISBN 9781427122063 (Electronic) | ISBN 9780778753841 (hardcover : alk. paper) | ISBN 9780778753971 (pbk. : alk. paper)
Subjects: LCSH: Space colonies--Juvenile literature. | Extraterrestrial bases--Juvenile literature.
Classification: LCC TL795.7 (ebook) | LCC TL795.7 .B69 2019 (print) | DDC 629.44/2--dc23
LC record available at https://lccn.loc.gov/2018050345

Crabtree Publishing Company

www.crabtreebooks.com   1-800-387-7650

Printed in the U.S.A./032019/CG20190118

Published in Canada
Crabtree Publishing
616 Welland Ave.
St. Catharines, Ontario
L2M 5V6

Published in the United States
Crabtree Publishing
PMB 59051
350 Fifth Avenue, 59th Floor
New York, New York 10118

Published in the United Kingdom
Crabtree Publishing
Maritime House
Basin Road North, Hove
BN41 1WR

Published in Australia
Crabtree Publishing
Unit 3 – 5
Currumbin Court
Capalaba QLD 4157

Contents

CHAPTER 1

Floating Among the Stars

Can you imagine living on another world? What would it be like to wake up and see the landscape of Mars from your bedroom window? How would it feel to float above the clouds of Venus? What would it be like to live on a **space station**, in **orbit** around Earth? For centuries, people have imagined traveling into space. Today, **astronomers**—scientists who study space—are asking themselves whether this might be possible.

What would it take for humans to live in space? Scientists have been considering the question ever since astronomers first realized Earth was a **planet** orbiting the Sun. As technology developed, scientists began figuring out how to leave Earth. In the later part of the 20th century, people used airplanes to fly toward the very edge of space. They learned that space is very different from the surface of our planet.

Space begins at the top of Earth's atmosphere, which is the envelope of gases that surrounds a planet.

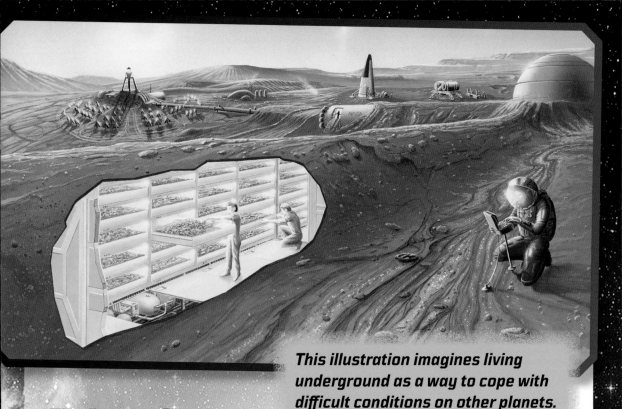

This illustration imagines living underground as a way to cope with difficult conditions on other planets.

The Race to Space

Starting in the second half of the 20th century, many scientists took up the challenge of getting people into space. Engineers worked to build rockets and other spacecraft that could leave Earth's atmosphere and safely return. **Astrophysicists** study the behavior of bodies in space. They figured out how space objects move in relation to one another, and how to send spaceships between two moving planets. **Astrobiologists** are scientists who study life on Earth, and potential life elsewhere. They wondered what life might be like on other planets and what humans would have to do to make it possible to live on other worlds.

Thanks to the work of such scientists, 12 people have walked on the Moon. More than 500 people have spent a combined total of 29,000 days in space. We have sent uncrewed missions to all the planets and some **dwarf planets** in our **Solar System**. Voyager 1, which was launched in 1977, is preparing to leave our Solar System altogether. We are a long way from being able to set up permanent **colonies** in space or on other planets, or make space travel common, but scientists are working on it. During your lifetime, you may be able to take a vacation on the Moon!

Earth provides us with everything we need to survive, so why would we leave our planet? Some scientists are proposing that we look for other worlds on which we could live because, one day, we will run out of **resources** on Earth. Resources are food, water, and energy sources such as coal and oil. Our population is growing each year, which means that we need more and more resources. Future populations will need to find these on other planets.

Signs of Life

When astrobiologists look for signs of life on other planets, they look for planets where liquid water can form. All life we know about needs water to survive. Even **cells**, which are the tiny building blocks of all living things, are mostly water. Water is so essential for living things that astrobiologists believe all planets that can support life must have water.

All life on Earth depends on water.

Habitable Zones

Earth is in our Solar System's "**Goldilocks Zone**." This zone is far enough from the Sun that water does not boil away, but not so far that all water freezes. It is also close enough to the Sun to receive warmth and light from its rays, but not so close that the rays scorch life on Earth. In these stable conditions, **ecosystems** have built up. Plants thrive in the sunlight, animals eat the plants, and humans eat the plants and animals. Earth is so perfect for life that it is called a Goldilocks Planet. Humans would need to find a planet very similar to Earth— another Goldilocks Planet—if they were to survive there.

Europa, a moon of Jupiter, releases jets of water that suggest it may have an ocean beneath its surface.

YOUR MISSION

We already know Earth is the only planet in our Solar System where conditions are just right for life to survive. If we find another Goldilocks Planet that we could live on, we could take plants and animals there from Earth. What plants and animals would you choose to take with you to a new Goldilocks Planet?

Why Do We Explore Space?

Exploration is part of human nature. People have traveled to almost every corner of our planet to find out more about it. From the 1400s, European explorers sailed along the coasts of Africa to the Indian Ocean, and across the Atlantic to the Caribbean, South America, and North America. These explorers discovered lands full of resources. They mapped the world and improved our understanding of Earth.

Pushing Boundaries

Curiosity, opportunity, and need drove early exploration. Today, they also drive many people's interests in exploring space. Humans have sent **probes**, or uncrewed spacecraft, to visit all eight planets in our Solar System, as well as to the dwarf planets Ceres and Pluto. **Satellites** in orbit above Earth have taught us a lot about our own planet. They have helped map our world more accurately than ever before.

For some people who are eager to explore, space might be a place where humans can find supplies of precious resources. They could mine rocky **asteroids** and **comets** for materials that are not easily found on Earth, or that occur only in small amounts.

The space probe Dawn visits the dwarf planet Ceres and the asteroid Vesta in this illustration.

Threats to Life on Earth

As scientists have learned more about Earth, they have realized that the planet may not be as stable as it seems. Asteroids have hit Earth in the past. Humans are now making big changes to our **environment** that may make it harder for us to live on the planet in the future. As our population grows, we are changing Earth's **climate** and running out of resources to keep us alive. We have also developed nuclear weapons, which are hugely destructive. People worry that humans could wipe themselves out if they began a nuclear war.

British **physicist** Stephen Hawking once said, "Humanity would likely not survive another 1,000 years without escaping beyond our fragile planet." The fact that all humans live on one planet means that the human race might become **extinct** if something disastrous happened to Earth. Even if we solve all the problems facing the human race today, our Sun will still burn through its fuel in 5 billion years. When that happens, it will expand to swallow Mercury and Venus, ending all life on Earth. At some point, if humans do not want all life to die out, they will have to find another home in space.

A nuclear war would fill the air with harmful radiation, making it difficult for any kind of life to survive.

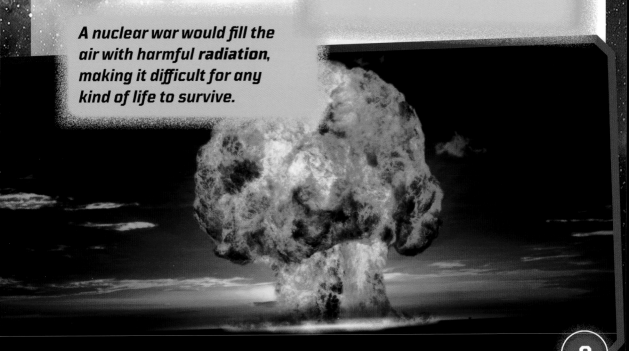

CHAPTER 2

Out of This World!

In the 1950s, the United States and the **Soviet Union** raced each other into space. Both wanted to make sure the other did not have control over what was called the "new frontier." On October 4, 1957, the Soviet Union launched Sputnik, the first artificial satellite to orbit Earth. On April 12, 1961, Soviet **cosmonaut** Yuri Gagarin became the first person to journey into space and return unharmed.

Leaving Earth

One of the biggest challenges about going into space is that Earth will not let us go without a fight! Objects leaving Earth must reach a speed of 6.95 miles per second (11.186 km/s) to overcome the pull of Earth's **gravity**. This is called **escape velocity**. Achieving such speeds requires a lot of **force**, or power. To deal with this problem, the National Aeronautics and Space Administration (NASA) built huge rockets such as the Saturn V, which can power into space. However, they require a lot of power to do so and can burn through 2,205,000 pounds (1,000,000 kg) of fuel in two minutes. Such large amounts of fuel can be dangerous, and many rockets have exploded during launch.

John Glenn became the first American to orbit Earth in 1962, onboard Friendship 7.

Another problem with space travel is the conditions astronauts face. In space, there is almost no **air pressure**, which is the weight of the air on everything. It is impossible to breathe. Moisture on the tongue, eyes, and skin boils, even though the temperature drops to –148 °Fahrenheit (–100 °C) in shadow. Direct sunlight can heat objects as high as 248 °Fahrenheit (120 °C).

Space's Deadly Toll

Returning from space is as dangerous as getting there. Spacecraft fall toward Earth at speeds of up to 17,400 miles per hour (28,000 kph). At that speed, the **friction**, or resistance caused by Earth's atmosphere, can heat a spacecraft's surface to 3,000 °Fahrenheit (1,650°C). **Heat shields**, which are surfaces that absorb heat, protect **capsules**, or the parts of spacecraft that hold the crew. As of 2018, of the 536 astronauts who have gone into space, 18 have died during spaceflight. Another 13 astronauts and test pilots have died during training and test flights.

The Soviet Union landed spacecraft on hard ground at the end of missions. Parachutes helped make the landing softer.

YOUR MISSION

When John Glenn orbited Earth in Friendship 7, the cabin was so small astronauts said, "You don't get in it, you put it on." Imagine what it would be like spending months or years traveling to another planet with other people in a space not much bigger than your bedroom. How would you make the experience easier?

U.S. astronaut Buzz Aldrin sets up an experiment during the first Moon landing in July 1969.

Up into Space!

As the United States and Soviet Union competed in the space race, they sent ships farther into our Solar System. Mariner 2 became the first **robotic** probe to fly past Venus in August 1962. Mariner 4 flew past Mars in November 1964. The United States continued its effort for superiority by planning to be the first to send people to the Moon. They succeeded with the Apollo 11 mission. On July 20, 1969, Neil Armstrong stepped off the **lunar module** Eagle onto the Moon's surface.

Staying Close to Home

After Apollo 11, people stepped on the Moon on five more occasions. No human has stepped on another world since. The cost of the space race was seen as too high. After the Moon, where else could people go? Mars seemed like the next frontier to many scientists, but at 33.9 million miles (54.7 million km), away, it is more than 182 times farther than the Moon. The United States and the Soviet Union focused on sending people into orbit around Earth instead.

The United States hoped to save money by building the space shuttle. This spacecraft could fly into space and back, then be reused.

Space Disasters

Space agencies also increasingly used robotic probes to explore space. These ships can go without water, food, or **oxygen**. This makes them lighter and easier to launch than a spacecraft carrying humans. Probes have given us our first views of the surfaces of Venus and Mars, as well as the **outer planets** of our Solar System: Jupiter, Saturn, Uranus, and Neptune.

Robotic probes are also used where possible because if a mission goes wrong, human lives are not lost. In 1986, the space shuttle Challenger exploded soon after launch, killing its seven crew members. In 2003, the Columbia space shuttle broke apart as it reentered Earth's atmosphere. Again, the crew all died.

Despite such accidents, it is inevitable that humans will have to travel into space. Humans can explore in ways robots cannot. If we are serious about building a human presence in space, we first need to send people there.

The robotic probe Galileo was launched in 1989. It visited Jupiter and its four large moons, Io, Europa, Ganymede, and Callisto.

We depend on gravity more than we think. Gravity is a force that pulls us toward Earth. We walk because gravity pulls us to the ground, and we push against the ground to walk. Without gravity, we would push up from the ground and not come back down! The simple act of walking is impossible in space, especially if there is nothing to push against. In space, people need special tools to move around.

Hold On!

Gravity does not disappear in Earth's orbit. Astronauts in orbit are constantly falling because of gravity, but everything around them is falling at the same speed. As a result, it feels as though astronauts are floating and weightless. In space stations, astronauts move around by grabbing things and pulling or pushing themselves along. Astronaut movement outside of a space station is called **extra-vehicular activity (EVA)**. For these difficult maneuvers, astronauts wear a special protective suit.

Suits Designed for Space

The suit that astronauts wear during an EVA provides an environment in which they can survive. The suit has to provide oxygen as well as prevent the astronaut from becoming too hot or cold. The suit must also allow astronauts to move around and use

During an EVA, an astronaut is held in place by a clamp at the end of a space arm.

tools in space. Astronauts flying the space shuttle wore suits that weighed 110 pounds (50 kg), with life-support backpacks weighing another 200 pounds (90 kg). While weight is less of a problem in the weightlessness of space, the suits are often very **rigid** and hard to move in. A new spacesuit is being designed by Boeing. It uses lighter and more flexible materials, and can make astronauts more comfortable. In the future, astronauts may wear skintight spacesuits, that provide enough pressure and heat to protect the body.

YOUR MISSION

Weightlessness affects more than just our movement. Imagine using a screwdriver in space. On Earth, your feet are held firmly to the ground so you can turn the screw with your hand. In space, unless you are holding onto something solid, the screw turns you! Can you imagine other things that are easy to do on Earth that would be more difficult in a weightless environment?

Space stations are designed to help humans live and work in space. They hold food, sleeping spaces, and work areas.

Salyut and Skylab

The Soviet Union launched the first space station, Salyut 1, in April 1971. The craft was launched as a single piece, 65 feet (20 m) long and 13 feet (4 m) in diameter. Once Salyut was in orbit, another spaceship joined it to deliver a crew of three. They stayed for 23 days on Salyut 1, which at that time was a record for the longest time in space. When they returned to Earth, however, a problem developed with their reentry capsule and all three men died. Despite the tragedy, other successful Salyut stations were launched later.

The first U.S. space station to orbit Earth was Skylab, launched in May 1973. Three crews visited between then and February 1974. They proved that humans could live and work in space for extended periods of time. At one point, they performed an emergency EVA to

Space stations use panels to gather energy from the Sun to generate electricity.

repair the panels that gathered sunlight to create electrical power. Although it was a success, Skylab was not big enough to be useful. It remained empty from 1974 until it fell from orbit in 1979.

A True Space Station

In 1986, the Soviet Union launched its new space station, Mir. This space station differed from earlier ones because it was built in pieces, which were each launched separately.

This allowed it to be larger than previous space stations. Crews took turns visiting it. Altogether, people were onboard Mir for a total of 3,644 days. The space station's residents included Valeri Polyakov, who still holds the record for the longest time an individual has spent on a single space mission, at 437 days and 18 hours. Mir orbited until 2001, when it was shut down and allowed to fall back to Earth.

MISSION:
Space Science

Objects in orbit move at least 4.3 miles per second (7 km/s). At these speeds, even tiny objects carry great force. In August 2016, a tiny piece of **debris** hit the Sentinel-1A satellite. It made a huge hole. Scientists worry that colliding **space junk** will create a cloud of debris that could endanger space flight from Earth. They are planning ways to clean up space junk to reduce the threat.

Astronauts in Skylab had wonderful views of Earth from space.

International Space Station

Today, the largest space station is the International Space Station (ISS). The first pieces were launched by NASA and foreign space agencies in 1998. The first crew members—Yuri Gidzenko, William Shepherd, and Sergei Krikalev —arrived on November 2, 2000, to live and work on the station as it orbited 254 miles (409 km) above Earth. Since then, more than 200 people have visited the ISS. The station is around 357 feet by 240 feet (109 m x 73 m), which is a bit larger than a football field. It has two bathrooms and living space comparable to a six-bedroom home.

Work in Orbit

The crew on the ISS perform many tasks as they orbit Earth. A lot of the work is science experiments that explore different ways we might live in space, such as investigating how plants and insects grow in weightless environments, or how long the station's equipment lasts. Ways of reusing water are being examined. New materials are being made in the **microgravity** environment, which is a place with very little gravity. They are then returned to Earth where they are compared to **samples**, or trial materials.

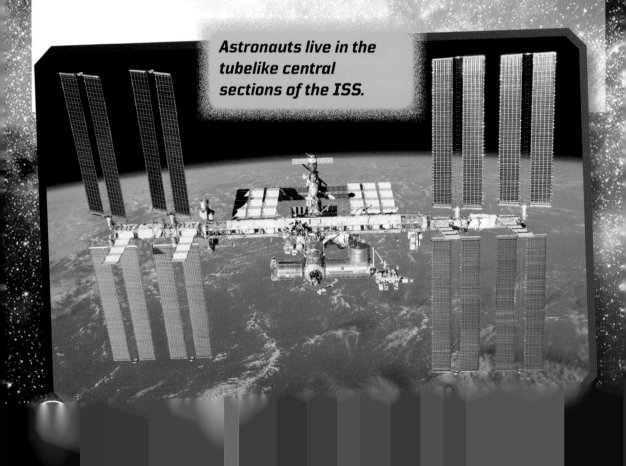

Astronauts live in the tubelike central sections of the ISS.

Human Experiments

ISS crews themselves are experiments. Physicians check their health in space and afterward to see how their bodies handle long periods in orbit. Muscles **atrophy**, or waste away, and grow weaker without the force of gravity to act against. Bones become less **dense**, or solid. Body fluids collect in the head rather than being pulled toward the feet, as they are on Earth. This can damage an astronaut's eyesight in space.

Astronaut Michael Foale uses a special microgravity laboratory for an experiment on the ISS.

Without the protection of Earth's atmosphere, astronauts are exposed to more **background radiation**, or energy waves that are everywhere in the universe. This can affect their cells. In 2018, NASA studied twins Mark and Scott Kelly. Scott spent a year on the ISS, while Mark stayed on Earth. When Scott came back, NASA scientists found that 7 percent of his **genes** had changed. Genes are chemical signals that pass on qualities from parents to their offspring. Such changes are something for scientists to consider as they plan missions to distant planets, where humans might be in space for two years or more.

MISSION:
Space Science

The ISS will eventually become too expensive to maintain. The U.S. government plans to stop funding the ISS after 2025. NASA will focus instead on missions to the Moon and Mars. China is building its own space station, which may start launching in 2020. Private companies such as Bigelow Aerospace are drawing up plans for their own space stations.

Permanent Settlements

Russian cosmonaut Valeri Polyakov holds the record for the longest single stay in space, at nearly 438 days. Although he exercised for two hours a day, his muscles wasted in the weightless environment. When he returned to Earth, he had difficulty walking. In space, bones also lose their strength and become easier to break.

The Spinning World

One solution to the astronauts' problems may be to build a space station shaped like a wheel. If the wheel spins like a spinning top, the rotation will create a **centrifugal** force, which is a force that pulls objects outward from the center of a spinning wheel. Astronauts would be pushed up against the outer wall of the space station, which would have an effect like that of gravity. The faster the spin, the heavier the **artificial**, or human-made, gravity that would be created.

The force created by the spinning would destroy existing space stations—they would break apart. For that reason, any space station intended to spin would have to be designed and built to be much stronger than existing stations. The same attention to design and build would need to be applied to long-range spaceships if people were to live in space for long periods of time. These spaceships would also need to spin.

This illustration shows part of the outer ring of a wheel-like space station. Although such structures have appeared in books and movies for decades, they have never been constructed in real life.

Some companies are looking at ways to take tourists into space. Between 2001 and 2009, Space Adventures sold tickets to the ISS onboard a Russian Soyuz spacecraft, for between $20-40 million. Seven space tourists made the flight. Virgin Galactic plans to build spaceplanes that can take tourists into orbit for $250,000. Although the planes are still being tested, more than 700 tickets have been sold. However, it will be some time before space travel is cheap enough for most people to afford.

In this illustration, a large elevator travels along a line connecting Earth to an orbiting space station.

Elevator to the Stars

Another option might be to tie orbiting space stations to Earth. Assuming it is possible to make strong enough materials, scientists and engineers have imagined a space station tied to Earth by a line more than 22,236 miles (35,786 km) long. The space station would be in **geostationary orbit**, meaning that it would always stay above the same spot on Earth as the planet rotates. Because of the centrifugal force created by Earth's spin, the space station would be spun outward, keeping the line tight. An elevator could be sent up and down the line to the space station, delivering people and supplies. The centrifugal force would create an effect similar to the **microgravity**, or small amounts of gravity, in the space station. A space elevator could deliver materials into orbit more easily and less expensively than large rockets.

Building a Moon Base

One of the first space objects humans might **colonize**, or settle on, is the Moon. It is the closest space object to Earth, and we know we can send people there. The Moon also has gravity, although it is only one-sixth that of Earth. There are many challenges to settling on the Moon, however. There is no atmosphere and no protection from the Sun's radiation. Temperatures range from –279 °Fahrenheit (-173 °C) in the dark to 260 °Fahrenheit (127 °C) in direct sunlight. However, buildings could provide an atmosphere and protection from the heat and cold. Underground chambers could provide large, comfortable living areas.

Our Amazing Moon

The pictures Apollo astronauts took of the Moon appear to show little more than rocks and dust, but appearances can be deceiving. Analysis of the Moon shows **oxides** of various metals, including iron, aluminum, magnesium, titanium, and silicon. A form of the **element** helium is also found in the Moon's surface. This form of helium is rare on Earth, but it is extremely valuable because it can be used to fuel **nuclear reactors**.

Astronauts would travel across the Moon in rovers, like the one shown in this illustration.

Future astronauts to the Moon will probably arrive in small landers at first.

Water on the Moon

Orbiting spacecraft using radar have located frozen water locked in the dust in **craters**, or depressions, near the Moon's **poles**, or its "top" and "bottom." In October 2009, NASA deliberately flew a probe into a crater, while sensors looked for water in the dust thrown up from the surface by the collision. The test confirmed that water was present, although it is still not clear how much. If there is enough, this water could supply a lunar colony. In addition, it could be split apart into **hydrogen** and oxygen, which are the gases often used as fuel to launch rockets.

MISSION:
Space Science

The Moon may provide more than just a place to mine resources. It could provide a gateway to the rest of our Solar System. The Moon's weaker gravity makes it easier to launch rockets from its surface. Large spaceships bound for Mars, Venus, or the outer Solar System could be built on the Moon. We would simply have to use special Earth–Moon shuttles to transfer to the Moon all the materials needed to build spaceships.

In recent years, space agencies other than NASA have begun to build spaceships. In the late 1990s, the XPrize Foundation was set up. It offered a prize of $10 million for any individual or private company that could fly a three-passenger craft 62 miles (100 km) into space twice within two weeks. The prize aimed to encourage private research into spaceflight, using ships that were cheaper to build than the usual rockets. The XPrize was won by Mojave Aerospace Ventures on October 4, 2004, when SpaceShipOne made its second successful flight. Since then, many private companies, such as SpaceX, have built rockets, launched satellites, and carried supplies to the ISS.

The Orion spaceship is being built to carry human crews on long missions.

NASA's Next Generation

With more private companies sending rockets into orbit, NASA has started working on a new generation of craft designed to travel deeper into space. Since 2011, NASA has worked with the private companies Lockheed Martin and Airbus to develop the Orion Multi-Purpose Crew Vehicle. This advanced spaceship is designed to carry a crew of up to six to the Moon, Mars, and even the **asteroid belt**. This area with many space rocks lies between the orbits of Mars and Jupiter. Extra supplies and life-support equipment for longer journeys could be supplied by an added module called a deep-space habitat.

Experimental Fuels

Rockets are still the best way scientists know of to beat Earth's gravity and launch spaceships into orbit. In the weightlessness of space, however, other methods of moving could be used.

An **ion thruster** uses electrically charged gas to propel it. This creates only a small amount of **thrust**, or pushing power, but the thruster can fire for a lot longer than rockets can. In weightlessness, even a small amount of thrust can push ships to great speeds. This has already been tried. Ion thrusters on the Dawn space probe increased the probe's speed by 6 miles per second (10 km/s). Larger ion thrusters could shorten the trip between Earth and Mars from months to as little as 39 days.

YOUR MISSION

Scientists are looking at various ways of launching spacecraft. One idea might be to build a large ramp. The spacecraft would be shot along it using high-powered magnets. An early plan for NASA's space shuttle had it being carried by a large plane to a high altitude, then firing rockets to head into space. If new launch plans are successful, how might they help us in our plans to further explore space?

Scientists drew up plans to launch the space shuttle from the back of an aircraft, but the technique was never tested.

A major problem of setting up homes in space is that conditions outside the colony buildings would be deadly. Colonists would live in fear of something going wrong and their protective environment being destroyed. Some scientists think it might be possible to overcome this problem through a process called **terraforming**. *Terra* is the Latin word for Earth. Terraforming is the process of making an unwelcoming planet such as Mars or Venus more like Earth, with air we can breathe and temperatures that can support human life.

This re-creation shows the surface of Mars as it may have appeared millions of years ago, with oceans of water and clouds in the sky.

Remaking Alien Worlds

Different planets would have to be terraformed in different ways. Mars has a very thin atmosphere, which prevents it from holding in the heat it receives from the Sun. Some scientists suggest forcing comets to crash into Mars. The comets would release gases and water vapor to add to the atmosphere. Large mirrors in orbit could reflect sunlight onto the surface, raising the temperature. Another idea would be to add **extremophile bacteria**, which can live in extreme conditions. They would release gases such as **carbon dioxide** and oxygen, adding to the thin Martian atmosphere.

On Venus, the thick clouds contain so much carbon dioxide, they trap too much of the Sun's heat. In 1991, British scientist Paul Birch suggested blasting this atmosphere with hydrogen.

The hydrogen would combine with the carbon dioxide to produce **graphite** and water. Another idea would be to use orbiting screens to block sunlight, cooling things down.

A Long-Term Plan

Such options would take centuries to make Venus or Mars ready for us to walk unprotected on their surfaces. The options sound like science fiction, but if we want to build a world that can house humans for thousands of years, we have to plan ahead.

MISSION:
Space Science

Terraforming a planet is a difficult task. Ecosystems on Earth are complex, with different plants and animals feeding off each other and supporting each other. It is easy for elements to be thrown out of balance. For example, mold unexpectedly started forming inside on the space station Mir. The mold rusted metal and caused a horrible smell. If humans try to terraform a planet so plants and bacteria will grow, astrobiologists will have to figure out ways to keep the process under control.

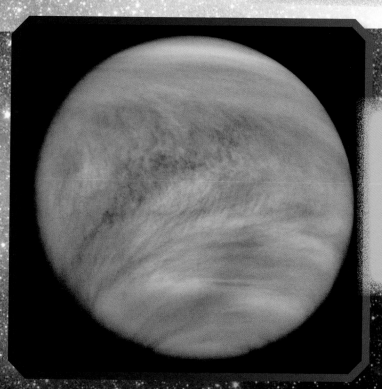

Venus is cloaked with thick clouds that swirl in huge weather patterns that make the planet's surface hostile for life.

Destination Mars

For many scientists, the next world for humans to visit should be Mars. Its distance from Earth ranges between 34–250 million miles (55–401 million km), while Venus ranges between 24–162 million miles (38–261 million km) away. Mars is a cold, rocky planet with a thin atmosphere and ice beneath its surface. In contrast, Venus is super-hot, with clouds of **sulfuric acid**, a chemical that dissolves many materials, and surface pressures equivalent to being at the bottom of the ocean.

Mars would not be an easy place to colonize. It is smaller than Earth and has just 38 percent of Earth's gravity. This means that a person who weighed 110 pounds (50 kg) on Earth would weigh 42 pounds (19 kg) on Mars. Humans would have to adjust to the lower gravity. It might be more difficult to walk, and their muscles might waste away. Mars is also colder than Earth, with temperatures averaging –67 ˚Fahrenheit (-55 ˚C). The thin carbon dioxide atmosphere is impossible for humans to breathe. Nothing could grow under these conditions.

On Mars, artificial gardens and farms could be built, in which scientists could grow food. This is Biosphere 2, which is a self-contained greenhouse building in the Arizona desert. The work carried out here could help scientists set up similar buildings on Mars.

This illustration shows astronauts on Mars. The illustration depicts the type of space vehicle that astronauts might use to travel across the planet.

A Place to Grow

One way to colonize Mars could be by building greenhouses. Glass buildings could allow sunlight through and keep oxygen inside. Colonists could grow crops on Martian soil using **fertilizer** brought from Earth or recycled from the waste of the colonists themselves. These crops would not only feed the colonists, but also help turn Mars's carbon dioxide into oxygen the colonists could breathe. In the early 1990s, scientists tested such a concept with Biosphere 2. It was too small to be **self-sufficient**, or able to support itself. However, over the long term, the model showed a possible first step toward adapting Mars into a planet that could support human life.

MISSION:
Space Science

Mars has no **magnetosphere**. On Earth, the magnetosphere protects our planet from the **solar wind**. The solar wind is a stream of electrically charged particles that flows constantly from the Sun into space. Scientists believe that Mars had an ocean and an atmosphere billions of years ago. Without a magnetosphere to protect them, however, the solar wind slowly ripped Mars's atmosphere and ocean out into space.

The view of Mars for the first colonists would look something like this image.

Missions to Mars

Robots have already visited Mars to find out more about it. From their visits, we have learned more about the planet than any other planet in our Solar System, apart from Earth. After several attempts, the lander Viking 1 arrived on August 20, 1975, followed by Viking 2 a few weeks later. The two landers sent home more than 50,000 photographs.

Starting in the 1990s, landers delivered rovers such as Sojourner, Opportunity, and Curiosity. They drove across the planet for years, analyzing the soil and sending back more than 350,000 images. In addition, the Mars Global Surveyor orbited the planet between 1997 and 2006, building an accurate map of the planet and revealing evidence that Mars once had oceans.

Plans are being made for more Mars missions. NASA's Mars 2020 will deliver a new rover to look for signs of ancient life. The vehicle will seek out the most interesting routes to drive. China, India, and the United Arab Emirates (UAE) have their own Mars missions planned.

The First Martians

NASA and others are also figuring out ways to send humans to Mars by 2040. NASA is planning missions to gather **data**, or information, for the trip. Trips to the ISS, for example, will show how spaceflight affects the human body. Other potential missions include plans to capture an asteroid and put it in orbit around the Moon. NASA would then send astronauts to the asteroid to build a base and live there for about the time it will take to travel to Mars.

Another approach is proposed by a group called Mars Direct. The idea is to send supplies to Mars first, followed by permanent settlers. Anyone who **volunteered** for this mission would not expect to come home to Earth. They would be expected to build a successful base on Mars—or die trying.

In this artwork from the 1950s, an artist imagines colonists mining the Martian moon Phobos for minerals.

YOUR MISSION

Based on what you have read in this book, what would it take to be a colonist on Mars? What jobs would you have to do to ensure the survival of the colony? What qualities, skills, and training do you think colonists might need? Give reasons for your answers.

It will take between 6–9 months for humans to reach Mars. Compared to travel to other planets, this is a short journey—but it is longer than any individual has ever spent in space. Packing enough food for even this relatively short journey is hard enough. Soon after they arrive, settlers would need to become self-sufficient. If humans hope to live on other planets for longer periods, we will need to find our own oxygen, water, and food there.

Growing Plants on Mars

We know Mars has water. The rovers found evidence of ice beneath the surface of the planet. However, growing food on Mars is not as simple as just planting seeds. Earth's soil is full of bacteria and **organic material**, or the remains of material that was once alive. They contain **nutrients**. Martian soil is crushed rock with no organic material, so plants do not grow well in it. Martian soil will need fertilizer to provide the nutrients that plants need to grow.

Plants are being grown in artificial environments on the ISS to help scientists figure out how they can grow them on Mars.

Growing plants in space is a huge challenge—but scientists are coming up with supersmart ways to do it.

Growing Without Soil

One solution to the poor Martian soil could be growing plants through **hydroponics**. This technique delivers nutrients directly to the roots of plants, allowing them to grow in liquids without soil. Astronauts on the ISS grew lettuce, peas, and radishes hydroponically and used the plants in their meals. Scientists have also grown potatoes and strawberries in this way. Hydroponic plants use less water and take up less space than plants grown in soil. Hydroponic laboratories are difficult to set up, however. They are often affected by bacteria, which travel easily between plants, causing them to die. The laboratories also need power to keep from drying out.

Hydroponics may be a good way for astronauts to grow food on spaceships during long journeys. It may be the best way to grow plants on planets and moons that have no suitable soil. Without food, our space missions will fail, so it is essential to investigate every way possible to make things grow and keep our astronauts fed.

CHAPTER 5

Beyond the Red Planet

In the next two decades, humans may start to live on the Moon and Mars. NASA and other space agencies do not plan to stop there, however. Although a lot of the current plans focus on the early days of setting up colonies, such as constructing places to live and welcoming the first arrivals, scientists are also looking at the next important steps.

An expert in human populations at the University of Florida calculated that to keep a stable population, a colony would need to have a minimum of 80 people. How do we ship that many people to a new colony? And once colonies on Mars and the Moon are thriving, where will the next frontiers be?

The Next Step

To answer some of these questions, NASA has set up a program called Next Space Technologies for Exploration Partnerships (NextSTEP). Once colonies are established, NASA believes it cannot be the only agency that provides flights between distant colonies and Earth.

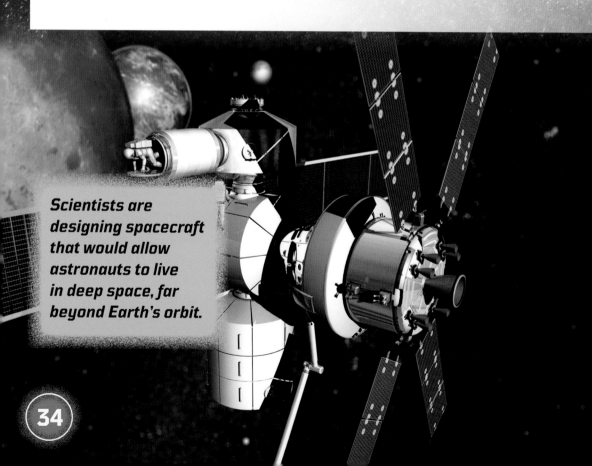

Scientists are designing spacecraft that would allow astronauts to live in deep space, far beyond Earth's orbit.

The Orion spaceships, as seen in this artist's impression, are intended to support crews for longer space journeys.

Working with private companies, NASA hopes to encourage new technologies that can improve on its Orion spacecraft. It wants to make it less expensive to launch, and able to carry people more efficiently.

Deep-Space Living

The Orion spacecraft are being designed to take people to the Moon and Mars. To get beyond Mars, NASA is working with other companies to design a spacecraft called the Deep Space Transport (DST). Using technologies tested on the ISS, DST could allow a crew to live and work in space for up to 1,000 days. It could take off from the Moon, saving fuel and bringing more of our Solar System in reach of human explorers.

MISSION: Space Science

Space is vast. Even the nearest star system to Earth, Alpha Centauri, is so far away that light from the star takes four years to reach us. The fastest ships that scientists can imagine will still take decades to reach the nearest stars. The people who board a spaceship to another world may do so realizing that it will be their children, not them, who will eventually step off the spaceship onto another world. Can you imagine setting off toward a planet that you will never see?

Humans may one day colonize the other planets of the inner Solar System, too. Even though Mercury has very little atmosphere to protect it from the Sun's heat, and its temperatures go from –279 °Fahrenheit (-173 °C) at night to 800 °Fahrenheit (427 °C) in the daytime, the fact that it is so close to the Sun means Mercury could become a major source of solar power. Power plants on Mercury would convert the Sun's light and heat into usable energy. However, scientists would need to figure out a way to beam the energy through space to Earth or to colonies on other planets. In 2012, NASA's MErcury Surface, Space ENvironment, GEochemistry, and Ranging mission (MESSENGER) probe confirmed that frozen water exists in craters at Mercury's poles. Scientists estimate there are billions of tons of ice at the poles that could supply hydrogen and oxygen, both for water for a colony and as ingredients for rocket fuel.

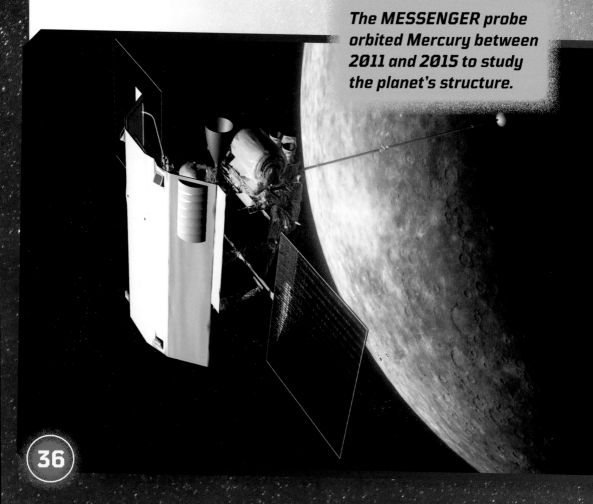

The MESSENGER probe orbited Mercury between 2011 and 2015 to study the planet's structure.

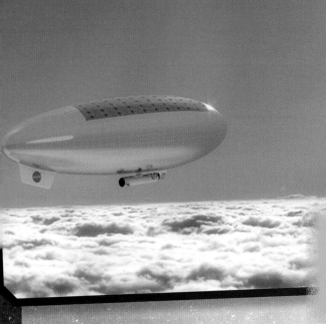

One way to deal with Venus's atmosphere might be for humans to live in balloons that would float above the planet.

Living in Hell

Venus was once imagined as a hot, jungle world, but space probes revealed a hellish landscape beneath the clouds. The atmosphere is mostly carbon dioxide, trapping the Sun's heat and raising temperatures to more than 842 ˚Fahrenheit (450 ˚C). The atmosphere of Venus is so thick it would feel unbearably heavy to humans.

The Cloud Riders

The atmosphere of Venus has destroyed every space probe sent there. And yet the planet might be easier to colonize than Mars. About 35 miles (55 km) above the surface of Venus, the clouds of sulfuric acid disappear and the pressure and temperature drop. The average temperature there is around 80 ˚Fahrenheit (27 ˚C), which is cool enough for liquid water to exist. The air pressure is similar to the pressure on the surface of Earth. The air is still carbon dioxide, but a balloon filled with the oxygen-nitrogen atmosphere of Earth would be able to float there. Some scientists have imagined building floating cities called HAVOCs (High Altitude Venus Operational Concept). When you consider the low temperatures, low air pressure, and low gravity of Mars, it might be easier to set up and live in floating cities high above the surface of Venus.

Beyond Mars, the distances between planets become even greater. Jupiter is a minimum of 365 million miles (587 million km) from Earth, and Saturn is nearly twice as far. Crossing these distances would be very difficult.

Ocean Moons

Humans are unlikely to ever be able to land on Jupiter and Saturn, which are both made up mainly of gas. However, the moons of both planets might offer possible sites for colonies.

Scientists are fascinated by Jupiter's moon Europa. It has a thin oxygen atmosphere and appears to have an icy surface over a huge ocean of water that may support life. In 1997, a private space group called the Artemis Project suggested that humans could colonize Europa by building a base on the surface and drilling into the icy crust. Pumping air beneath the ice could create a bubble in which buildings could be constructed. The icy crust would protect the colony against radiation.

The surface of Europa is covered in ice. Beneath this surface could be an ocean—perhaps one with life in it already!

Another moon of Jupiter that interests scientists is Callisto. In 1997, the Galileo probe showed there was ice on its surface, and perhaps an ocean 60 miles (97 km) below. A NASA study in 2003 suggested a human colony could be built on the surface of Callisto. It could use the moon's resources to produce rocket fuel for ships heading even farther out into our Solar System.

Saturn Possibilities

Saturn has as many as 62 moons, among which scientists are most interested in Enceladus. This icy moon may have a liquid ocean beneath its surface. It may also support life. Saturn's moon Titan, meanwhile, is 50 percent larger than Earth's Moon. Although it is very cold, it has a climate and weather. It also has rivers, lakes, and seas, made mainly of liquid **methane**, which exists naturally as a gas on Earth. Titan has all the materials needed for human life. It could be terraformed using mirrors to reflect more sunlight onto the surface. This would trap heat in Titan's atmosphere, which would warm its surface to a more comfortable temperature.

Sunlight catches the atmosphere of Titan, which is mostly nitrogen, with clouds of methane and ethane.

MISSION:
Space Science

In the future, ships could be sent to mine the asteroid belt. Asteroids contain raw materials such as gold, iridium, silver, platinum, and tungsten that could be shipped to Earth. Other metals, such as iron, cobalt, nickel, and aluminum, could be used to build bases on asteroids for miners to live. The rewards are potentially huge. The asteroid Anteros, for example, might contain up to $1,250 billion in magnesium, aluminum, and iron.

What's Next?

Space exploration has advanced a long way in a short period of time. It took about 20 years from the launch of the first successful space rocket for the U.S. astronauts Neil Armstrong and Buzz Aldrin to reach the Moon in 1969. Since then, we have put hundreds of people and thousands of satellites in orbit around Earth. Space probes have revealed secrets from all the planets and their moons, from the intense heat and pressure on Venus to the huge oceans beneath the icy crusts of Europa and Enceladus.

Robot landers have discovered a lot of information about Mars. However, the last time a human stepped onto another world was December 19, 1972, when Apollo 17 landed on the Moon. Humans have not been back to the Moon since. We know the future success of the human race depends on space colonization, so it is essential that we develop the science and technology needed to make this possible. NASA agrees. It is working on plans to send people back to the Moon and for the first time to Mars, possibly by 2040.

Robotic space travel has come a long way since astronauts explored the Moon—yet no humans have visited the Moon or other space bodies for nearly 50 years.

MISSION:

Space Science

If it is not possible to change a planet to support human life, it may be easier to change humans. We would do this by changing our genes. Genes carry the instructions that tell cells how to develop in new organisms. We might be able to change human genes to make people able to live in places with high levels of radiation or adapt our bone and muscles to handle low- or high-gravity environments. However, some people wonder whether, if we change our genes, would we still be human?

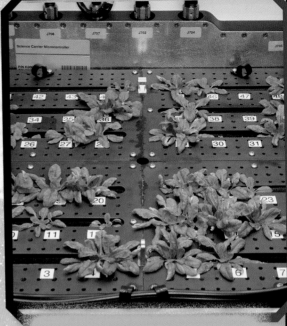

Scientists have learned how to change the genes of plants so they can adapt to new environments. Could they now apply that science to human genes?

The European Space Agency (ESA), Russia, and China are all moving their own space programs forward. For many experts, the question is not if humans will step onto another planet, but when.

To the Stars

Beyond Mars, possibilities exist for human colonies on some of the moons of Jupiter and Saturn. Beyond that again, scientists hope we may one day send spacecraft to our neighboring star systems. There are 250 billion stars in the Milky Way **galaxy**. By November 2018, astronomers using high-powered space telescopes had identified 3,826 **exoplanets**, or planets orbiting other stars. A number of these exoplanets are nearly the size of Earth and orbit in their stars' "Goldilocks Zones." Perhaps one of these planets could become a future home in space for humankind.

As we advance into our Solar System, how might this affect life on Earth? The technology that put people on the Moon helped improve the daily lives of nearly everyone. The computer that got Apollo 11 to the Moon was less powerful than a laptop or smartphone today. But the research that went into creating it made future generations of computers possible. Satellites orbiting Earth have helped us map our planet better. The Global Positioning System (GPS), which keeps us from getting lost, uses a network of satellites. Communications satellites make it easier for us to talk to people halfway around the world.

Earth and Its Colonies

If humans start setting up colonies on other planets and sending people to live there permanently, what relationship will settlers in those colonies have with Earth? Would space colonies simply be the source of resources for Earth, or might they eventually become so large and powerful that they one day claim independence from Earth? And what of future generations of colonists on those planets? Will their children be able to decide their own futures, or will they have to do whatever people on Earth tell them to do?

Could the future of Mars include independence? Would Earthlings who colonize the planet, like the explorer in this illustration, call themselves Martians?

Natural sites such as this Australian waterfall might benefit if industry moved to other planets because Earth's air and water would be kept cleaner.

The Future of Earth

If humans set up successful colonies in space, it might be possible to move **polluting**, or dirty, industries to other planets. This might enable a cut in pollution on Earth and a reduction in the dangerous gases, called **greenhouse gases**, that trap the Sun's heat in the atmosphere. Perhaps Earth might become a **nature reserve**, where the environment is left alone to thrive in its natural state. Perhaps one day, rather than sending tourists from Earth into space, the tourists will be visitors from space colonies who make a trip to Earth to see where the human race began. Anything is possible—as long as humans continue to explore setting up a home in space.

YOUR MISSION

Imagine you are a space tourist in a future in which people have colonized our Solar System. Which planets would you most like to visit? Which planets would you want to avoid? Would you want to leave Earth and become a colonist on another planet? Why, or why not? Give reasons for your answer.

Your Space Science Mission

You have read about how scientists around the world have learned about the planets in our Solar System. Humans have sent robots to explore all of them, plus other space objects such as comets, asteroids, and dwarf planets. You have also learned about how the drive to explore has led humans into the unknown since the creation of the human race itself. Today, that same drive to explore is shaping future space missions. Scientists are planning how to put people on Mars and how to set up larger colonies on other bodies in space. Now it is your chance. Your mission is to figure out how to set up a colony elsewhere in our Solar System. Who knows, your mission might change the entire future of the human race!

If you could settle in space, where would you choose? How would you shape that world?

Planning Your Mission

Flying saucer

1 Think about what you want to achieve.
Do you want to send people to live on a space station, or to build a colony on an asteroid? Or would you prefer to start terraforming another planet? Think about your aims. Do you want to mine space bodies for resources, or set up a permanent new home for humankind?

2 Choose a target.
The planets and other bodies of our Solar System are vastly different. They range from the hot, thick atmosphere of Venus to the cold, thin air of Mars. Research the planets and their moons to see which might be suitable for human life. Do not forget to consider how far they are from Earth, and how long traveling there would take.

3 Design your mission.
What are the first steps you would take? Would you send humans on long voyages into space, or would you start by sending robot spacecraft? Once you have made contact with another world, what are the next steps?

4 Plan for the long term.
Making a home in space will take decades. What new technologies would you develop to help colonists grow food, for example, or to alter human genes for space survival?

5 Choose your crews.
When it is time to send people into space, who should go? Would you send science experts or soldiers skilled at survival techniques? Would it be better to send families whose children will live on in your colony?

6 Collaborate!
Once you have some ideas jotted down, share them with a friend. See if they can come up with suggestions and new ideas to add to yours.

MARS MISSION
ADVENTURE
20 30
EXPEDITION

Glossary

Please note: Some **bold-faced** words are defined where they appear in the book.

asteroids Small rocky bodies that orbit the Sun

bacteria Tiny organisms that may cause disease

carbon dioxide A gas breathed out by humans and used by plants to make energy

climate The usual weather conditions of a place

colonies Settlements set up beyond the homeland of their inhabitants

comets Bodies made of ice and dust that travel around the Sun

cosmonaut A Russian astronaut

debris Pieces of trash

dwarf planets Bodies that orbit a star but are not large enough to be considered planets

ecosystems Groups of plants and animals that live and interact together

element A chemical that cannot be broken down

environment What makes up our surroundings

extinct No longer existing

extremophile A form of life that can live in extreme conditions

fertilizer A substance added to soil to help plants grow

galaxy A cluster of billions of stars held together by gravity

graphite A form of the element carbon

gravity A force that attracts all objects toward one another

lunar Related to the Moon

magnetosphere The region surrounding a planet such as Earth in which the planet's magnetic field is the dominant magnetic field.

module A detachable part of a spacecraft

moon Space body that orbits a planet

nuclear reactors Machines that generate electricity from nuclear reactions

nutrients Substances that provide energy for living things

orbit A path taken by one body around another

oxides Substances created when oxygen combines with a metal

oxygen A colorless gas humans use to breathe

physicist Someone who studies the physical qualities of things

planet Large body in space that orbits a star

radiation A harmful form of energy that travels as waves

resources Useful materials

rigid Stiff and unmoving

robotic Able to perform mechanical tasks based on programmed instructions

satellites Natural or artificial objects that orbit a planet or other body in space

solar system A star and all the bodies that orbit it

Soviet Union A large communist country that existed in Eastern Europe and Asia from 1922 to 1991. It was dominated by what is now Russia.

space junk Human-made objects floating in space

space station An orbiting spacecraft used for long-term missions

volunteered Freely offered to do something

Learning More

Books

Hamilton, John. *International Space Station: The Science Lab in Space* (Xtreme Spacecraft). ABDO Publishing, 2017.

Hawksett, David. *Living on Mars: Can You Colonize a Planet?* (Be a Space Scientist!). PowerKids Press, 2018.

Hogan, Christa C. *Space Stations* (Destination Space). Focus Readers, 2018.

Jefferis, David. *Space Colonists: Living on New Worlds.* (Our Future in Space). Crabtree Publishing Company, 2018.

Williams, Dr. Dave, and Loredana Cunti. *Destination: Space: Living on Other Planets* (Dr. Dave—Astronaut). Annick Press, 2018.

Websites

This site has many quizzes, games, and videos about our Solar System and space exploration designed for young readers:
   kidsastronomy.com

Go here to learn about the challenges of exploring Mars and what its future might be:
   mars.nasa.gov/participate/funzone

NASA has loads of details for young people about space travel and our Solar System:
   spaceplace.nasa.gov/menu/play

Want to find out about life in space and our place in the universe? Try this website:
   www.esa.int/esaKIDSen

Index

About the Author

James Bow has written many books for children, from geography and science to history and topical debate. He has written a number of books about space science, which is one of his favorite topics.